# AI Copywriting for Ads

## Write Converting Headlines, Captions, and Hooks Instantly

*By Joe Correa*

Published by Live Stronger Faster



First Edition

# Table of Contents

# Introduction

In the digital marketing landscape, the most powerful weapon a business can wield isn't always the biggest ad budget or the most advanced algorithm—it's words. The right words have the power to stop a scrolling thumb, spark curiosity, trigger emotion, and convert attention into action. This book, *AI Copywriting for Ads*, is your guide to mastering that power using the most advanced AI tools available today. From crafting magnetic headlines to writing emotionally charged captions and scroll-stopping hooks, you'll learn how to merge human psychology with artificial intelligence to create copy that sells effortlessly.

We've entered an era where AI can generate ideas, test variations, and analyze performance faster than any human could. But the real magic happens when human creativity directs that intelligence with strategic intent. AI tools like ChatGPT, Jasper, Copy.ai, and others can now understand tone, intent, and even emotional nuance—yet they still require a skilled marketer to guide the process. That's where you come in. Throughout this book, you'll learn how to become the *creative director* of AI copywriting, combining proven persuasion frameworks with AI's ability to generate endless variations in seconds. The goal isn't to replace human creativity; it's to amplify it—to make your ideas sharper, your testing faster, and your conversions higher.

Consider the difference between an average ad and a viral one. The average ad uses generic language—"Buy now," "Limited offer," "Don't miss out." The viral ad, on the other hand, speaks directly to emotion and identity—"Stop wasting hours scrolling when you could be building your dream life," or "Your future self will thank you for clicking this." AI can now analyze millions of these high-performing phrases across industries, learning what works best for each audience segment. As a marketer, this gives you superpowers. Instead of guessing what your audience will respond to, you can let data-driven AI models test and refine every line for maximum impact.

In the first section of this book, you'll discover how to train AI to write in your *brand voice*—whether that's professional, playful, luxury, or lifestyle-oriented. You'll learn prompt frameworks that generate copy consistent with your mission, values, and tone across every ad platform. From Facebook headlines to Instagram captions, YouTube scripts to TikTok hooks, every word your audience sees should sound unmistakably like *you*. You'll also explore how to analyze your competitors' copy to uncover hidden emotional triggers that their audiences respond to—and then teach AI to replicate that style while keeping your unique brand identity intact. Next, we'll dive into AI ad prompts and copy formulas that are proven to convert. You'll explore timeless frameworks like AIDA (Attention, Interest, Desire, Action), PAS (Problem, Agitation, Solution), FAB (Features, Advantages, Benefits), and storytelling-based models that blend perfectly with AI tools. I'll show you how to input structured prompts that produce multiple headline and caption options instantly—saving you hours of brainstorming while maintaining professional, persuasive quality. You'll also learn how to instruct AI to analyze tone and emotional depth, ensuring your copy matches your audience's mood and intent—whether it's excitement, aspiration, curiosity, or urgency.

Beyond creation, this book will also show you how to use AI for *copy optimization*. Modern ad platforms reward relevance and engagement, not just flashy visuals. AI tools can now measure word choice, emotional tone, and semantic similarity to identify which ad copy performs best. We'll discuss how to use these analytics to continuously refine your text, test new variations, and maintain peak performance across campaigns. Imagine running ten versions of the same headline overnight and waking up to find which one generated the highest click-through rate, engagement, and conversion—all without lifting a finger. That's what AI-powered copywriting makes possible.

You'll also uncover how to write high-performing *hooks*—the critical first line that determines whether your viewer keeps scrolling or clicks through. Using natural language models, you'll learn to train AI to mimic top-performing hooks across industries, adapting them for your own offers. You'll see how a single well-written line like "What if you could triple your results without spending another dollar on ads?" can outperform an entire paragraph of traditional copy. Hooks are psychological levers, and AI helps you identify which levers work best for your target audience based on their behavior, preferences, and pain points.

In today's marketing ecosystem, personalization is the new persuasion. With AI, you can now create custom ad versions for every audience segment—each with tailored headlines, pain points, and emotional tones. This book will show you how to use AI to generate adaptive copy that automatically aligns with each viewer's stage in the buying journey. Cold leads might see ads that spark curiosity; warm leads might get reassurance and proof; and hot leads might see offers with urgency and exclusivity. The result is higher conversions, lower ad costs, and a brand experience that feels human even when powered by AI.

One of the most exciting aspects of AI copywriting is the rise of *emotional AI*—tools that can detect and predict emotional response through text. Imagine having an assistant that tells you which version of your ad is more likely to inspire trust, curiosity, or excitement. Throughout this book, you'll see how emotional intelligence can be built into your ad prompts, transforming ordinary copy into emotionally resonant storytelling that connects instantly. You'll also learn ethical principles for AI copywriting—how to use persuasion responsibly, avoid manipulation, and create messages that empower your audience instead of exploiting them.

Finally, we'll explore how AI copywriting fits into the future of marketing careers and entrepreneurship. As automation becomes mainstream, businesses will no longer compete on who writes faster—they'll compete on *who prompts better*. Those who understand how to communicate with AI tools effectively will dominate digital marketing, freelancing, and eCommerce. Whether you're a business owner, marketer, or content creator, learning how to direct AI to produce persuasive copy will become one of the most profitable skills of this decade.

By the time you finish this book, you'll know exactly how to transform a blank screen into a full library of ad copy that converts. You'll have frameworks, prompt templates, emotional analysis tools, and optimization systems that let you produce more in one day than most teams do in a week. The age of AI-powered creativity isn't about replacing human writers—it's about giving every marketer the ability to think bigger, test smarter, and sell faster. Your next viral campaign could be just one perfect AI-generated headline away. Welcome to *AI Copywriting for Ads: Write Converting Headlines, Captions, and Hooks Instantly*—your blueprint for mastering persuasive communication in the AI era.

# Chapter 1: The Birth of AI Copywriting (From Human Intuition to Machine Intelligence)

For decades, marketing success depended on intuition, experience, and trial and error. The art of copywriting was once considered an almost mystical craft—a delicate balance of psychology, rhythm, and timing that separated average ads from legendary ones. Advertising icons like David Ogilvy and Eugene Schwartz built entire empires on words that could move millions. But as we entered the digital age, something changed. Attention spans shortened, platforms multiplied, and competition for every second of consumer focus grew fierce. The result was a marketing landscape where speed, adaptability, and precision became just as important as creativity. And out of that pressure, *AI copywriting* was born.

AI copywriting is not simply about generating words—it's about creating impact faster and smarter than ever before. With natural language processing (NLP) and large language models like ChatGPT, Jasper, and Copy.ai, marketers can now analyze what emotionally resonates with their audience, replicate successful phrasing patterns, and instantly adapt tone and structure to any platform. Instead of spending hours brainstorming, professionals can now use AI to create dozens of ad versions, each crafted for specific emotions—trust, curiosity, urgency, or desire. But while AI provides speed, it's still the human behind the keyboard who defines the *direction*. The human marketer remains the storyteller, strategist, and brand voice architect guiding the machine.

The evolution of AI copywriting can be understood in three major phases. The first was **automation**, where AI began handling repetitive tasks such as keyword generation or A/B testing ad headlines. The second was **augmentation**, where AI became a true assistant—helping copywriters brainstorm ideas, rewrite paragraphs, and adapt tone to match specific personas. The third phase—the one we're in now—is **co-creation**, where AI doesn't just follow commands but collaborates. Through prompting, marketers can engage in a creative conversation with the model, refining ideas until they align perfectly with strategy, data, and emotion.

What makes AI copywriting revolutionary is its ability to combine **data and psychology**. Traditional copywriters relied on instinct to guess what worked. AI tools now analyze billions of data points from successful ads across industries, revealing the exact emotional triggers that generate engagement. They can determine whether "you deserve better" performs stronger than "take control today," or whether a headline using scarcity ("Only 3 spots left") outperforms one that uses empowerment ("Start your next chapter now"). This shift allows marketers to replace intuition-based copy with evidence-based storytelling.

But the real magic happens when AI learns your **brand voice**. Every company has a unique tone—some are bold and daring, others calm and trustworthy, others witty and conversational. AI can be trained through examples of your existing ads, website copy, and customer emails to match that exact voice. Once trained, it becomes a creative partner capable of generating copy that sounds human, natural, and consistent with your brand across every channel. The more you feed it, the smarter and more personalized it becomes.

One of the most misunderstood aspects of AI copywriting is that it's *not* about replacing writers—it's about empowering them. In the same way that a calculator didn't replace mathematicians, AI won't eliminate copywriters; it will make them exponentially more capable. It eliminates creative fatigue, helps overcome writer's block, and accelerates testing cycles. You no longer need to spend half your day agonizing over a headline. With AI, you can generate 20 alternatives in seconds, analyze predicted engagement, and choose the winner based on data instead of guesswork.

To use AI effectively, marketers must develop a new skill: **prompt engineering**. The prompt is the new brief. It defines the tone, intent, emotion, and direction of your ad. For example, a simple prompt like "Write a Facebook ad for a weight-loss app" will yield something generic. But a powerful prompt like "Write a persuasive Facebook ad headline and caption targeting busy parents who want to lose weight without dieting, using an empathetic tone and focusing on freedom rather than guilt" will produce something infinitely more compelling. The difference lies in specificity. The more context you give AI, the better it performs.

As AI continues to evolve, it's also beginning to understand **emotion**. Emotional AI models can predict how your copy will make readers feel and how that emotion affects their decision-making. This means you can design ads that don't just inform—they move. An AI-powered system can now tell you which words evoke trust, excitement, or curiosity in real time. For marketers, this represents the ultimate competitive advantage: the ability to scale empathy.

However, with great power comes responsibility. Ethical copywriting still matters. Using AI to manipulate or mislead customers erodes trust and damages your brand long-term. The best AI copywriting follows transparency, authenticity, and respect for the consumer's intelligence. In this book, you'll learn how to build trust-driven messages that convert through value and clarity, not pressure.

The next time you scroll through your social media feed, pay attention to which ads stop you. Chances are, they share three things: clarity, emotional resonance, and rhythm. Whether you realize it or not, many of those ads were written—or at least optimized—by AI. The future of advertising isn't about man versus machine; it's about synergy. The human brain understands empathy, context, and cultural nuance, while AI provides data, speed, and scale. Together, they create the most powerful marketing force in history.

By the end of this chapter, you should see AI copywriting not as a technical shortcut, but as a creative amplifier. It's the next stage in the evolution of human communication—a way to tell your brand story with precision, persuasion, and purpose. The words you write with AI will reach millions faster, speak deeper, and convert higher. The key is learning how to speak *to* the machine so that it speaks *for* you.

### *Lena's Human Intuition*

Lena sat in front of her laptop, the soft hum of her desk light casting a warm circle over the keyboard. She had written ads for nearly a decade—Facebook, Instagram, Google—you name it. She'd seen every trend come and go: clickbait headlines, emotional storytelling, minimalist captions. But lately, she felt exhausted. The pace of digital marketing had become relentless. Clients demanded ten ad versions in a single day, each one perfectly targeted and emotionally tuned. Her creativity was stretched thin. She opened her notes and stared at the blinking cursor, that silent reminder of pressure.

Then she tried something new. A colleague had mentioned an AI tool that could "write like a human." Skeptical but curious, she opened ChatGPT and typed: *"Write five ad headlines for a skincare brand that promotes confidence and natural beauty, in an empowering tone."* Within seconds, the screen filled with options. "Glow isn't something you buy—it's something you feel." "Your skin tells your story—make it a beautiful one." "Confidence looks good on you." Lena blinked. These were good—really good. Not perfect, but good enough to make her sit up straighter. She felt a spark of excitement she hadn't felt in months.

She began testing. Each morning, she'd feed the AI new prompts—different tones, target audiences, product angles. Within a week, her productivity tripled. Her clients noticed. Engagement rates rose, conversions followed, and soon her inbox overflowed with new opportunities. But what surprised her most wasn't the efficiency—it was how much *better* she'd become as a writer. The AI wasn't replacing her voice; it was sharpening it. It forced her to think in structure, in psychology, in clarity. It made her dissect what truly moved people. One evening, while sipping tea, Lena reflected on how much the field had changed. When she first started, copywriting was like alchemy—a mix of instinct and inspiration. She'd spend hours reading old ad books, studying the masters, trying to understand what made "Just Do It" or "Think Different" so timeless. Now, with AI, she had access to a digital library of collective human persuasion. The machine had become a mentor—analyzing, refining, suggesting. Yet the soul of the message still came from her.

She remembered one campaign that proved it. A mental health startup hired her to craft an ad about overcoming burnout. The AI-generated drafts were technically flawless but emotionally flat. So Lena rephrased the prompt: *"Write as if you're talking to a friend who's pretending they're okay."* The output stunned her. "You don't have to keep pretending. Rest isn't weakness—it's renewal." That line became the campaign's centerpiece. Thousands shared it. The startup doubled its sign-ups in a week. And for the first time, Lena realized AI could do more than write—it could *listen.*

Months later, Lena launched her own agency—half human, half machine. She trained her AI assistant on her writing style, tone, and portfolio. Soon, clients began calling her "the copy whisperer." She wasn't faster because of AI—she was freer. She had time to focus on strategy, storytelling, and emotion while the AI handled variations, analytics, and testing. She was doing twice the work in half the time, and loving it.

But not everyone understood. At a marketing conference, a fellow writer confronted her: "Aren't you afraid AI will take your job?" Lena smiled. "Only if I stop leading it," she replied. "AI doesn't replace creativity—it scales it." She explained how AI had become her collaborator, not her competitor. How it analyzed emotional tone, optimized structure, and even predicted which line would convert best—yet still relied on her human intuition to feel what was *right*.

By the end of her presentation, even skeptics were curious. They asked for her prompts, her workflow, her results. That day, Lena realized something profound: the future of copywriting wasn't about man versus machine—it was about partnership. AI could process infinite data, but only humans could infuse meaning. Together, they could create messages that reached deeper than either could alone.

Years later, Lena still begins every campaign the same way: by opening her AI assistant and typing, *"Let's write something that makes people feel again."* And every time, as the words begin to form on the screen, she smiles. The blinking cursor no longer feels like pressure—it feels like possibility. The art of copywriting had evolved, but its essence remained unchanged: connection, empathy, and truth. The tools had changed, but the mission—to move hearts and minds—never would.

# Chapter 2: Understanding Persuasion (The Psychology Behind Every Word)

Every great piece of ad copy, no matter the platform, begins with one question: *Why do people buy?* The surface answer—"because they need something"—is too simple. People don't buy products; they buy feelings. They buy the sense of confidence, security, belonging, or transformation that the product promises. This is why psychology sits at the heart of persuasive copywriting. AI tools may be able to generate the words, but understanding *why* those words work is the skill that separates marketers who make noise from those who make impact.

When writing ads with or without AI, you're essentially communicating with the human subconscious. Over 90% of buying decisions are emotional before they are logical. A person might justify a purchase later with logic, but the initial spark is always emotional. The desire to feel special, to save time, to reduce stress, or to be admired—these are the invisible forces that drive consumer behavior. Your job as a copywriter is to understand which emotional switch to activate for your audience.

In AI copywriting, psychology becomes data. Modern models have been trained on billions of pieces of text, from high-performing ads to social media captions that went viral. This data allows them to recognize language patterns associated with emotional engagement. For example, words like *exclusive, proven, secret, new, unlock,* or *discover* trigger curiosity and desire. Phrases like *finally achieve, take control, or transform your life* evoke empowerment. AI doesn't just guess—it statistically analyzes what consistently drives response. When you learn how to guide these insights with precise prompts, you can shape AI into a psychological copywriting engine.

To master persuasive AI copywriting, you must understand the three layers of influence: **emotion, logic, and trust.** Emotion grabs attention, logic justifies the purchase, and trust removes resistance. Imagine you're selling a business credit course. An emotional opening line might be, "Stop letting banks decide your financial destiny." The logical follow-up could be, "Learn how to access up to $100,000 in business credit without using personal guarantees." And trust is built by adding proof: "Join over 10,000 entrepreneurs who've already done it." AI can write each of these parts—but only you can determine the balance.

Another key concept in persuasive writing is **framing**. Framing defines how an offer is perceived. For instance, instead of saying "Pay $299 for the course," you might say,

"Invest less than a dollar a day in a skill that can change your financial future." Both communicate the same price, but the second reframes the cost as an investment and positions the benefit upfront. When prompting AI, framing can be taught by including emotional context: *"Reframe the price as a life-changing opportunity instead of a payment."* The AI will adapt its word choice accordingly.

You should also understand **pain and pleasure psychology.** Every ad either moves a person away from pain or toward pleasure. Pain-based copy highlights what the customer wants to avoid—debt, confusion, failure, wasted time. Pleasure-based copy highlights what they want to achieve—freedom, peace of mind, wealth, recognition. The most powerful campaigns often blend both. For example, "Tired of writing ads that get ignored? Let AI help you write captions that get clicked, saved, and shared." Here, pain (being ignored) and pleasure (being seen and successful) coexist to create balance.

AI models can be directed to write in this dual tone by using prompts that describe *emotion* explicitly. For instance, "Write ad copy that starts with a relatable frustration and transitions into an empowering promise." This instructs AI to simulate the emotional rhythm of a real conversation—beginning with empathy, moving toward hope, and ending with action. That pattern mirrors how humans process persuasion: feel understood → see possibility → act.

Beyond emotion and logic, the next psychological pillar is **social proof**. People trust what others have already validated. That's why testimonials, case studies, and data points make ad copy exponentially stronger. When prompting AI, you can simulate this by adding credibility lines: "Include a sentence showing the number of users, success stories, or community impact." Even if you plan to replace the numbers later, AI will frame the ad to sound authoritative.

Finally, we must address the psychology of **simplicity.** In today's world of information overload, clarity converts. A confused mind doesn't buy. Great copy simplifies choices, highlights one transformation, and ends with one clear call to action. When prompting AI, always include brevity cues: *"Write in short, emotional sentences that flow like spoken conversation."* The result feels more natural and persuasive. Remember, simple doesn't mean basic—it means strategic. Every word either moves the reader closer to the goal or away from it.

The deeper you understand persuasion, the more powerful your AI prompts become. AI can generate endless words, but it needs human direction to strike emotional chords that truly resonate. When you combine your understanding of psychology with AI's precision, you move from writing copy to orchestrating emotion. You stop selling products and start shaping perceptions. And that is the secret to creating ads that don't just get clicks—they get remembered.

### *Miles True Meaning Behind Every Word*

Miles leaned back in his chair, staring at the ad dashboard on his screen. The results weren't bad, but they weren't great either. Click-through rates hovered around 1.8%. For weeks, he had been testing headlines and captions using AI, but something was missing. His ads looked professional, the copy was clean, the visuals sharp—but people weren't feeling it. He could sense it in the comments. Too technical. Too robotic. Too safe.

One night, frustrated, he revisited an old notebook from his first marketing job. Inside were scribbled notes from a seminar he'd attended years ago. On the first page, written in bold letters, were the words: *"People don't buy products. They buy emotions."* He stared at it for a long moment. That's what had been missing. His ads were informative, but they didn't touch people. They didn't speak to pain or hope—they just sold features.

The next morning, Miles decided to experiment. He opened ChatGPT and wrote: *"Write a Facebook ad headline for a freelancer course that helps people escape 9-to-5 jobs. Focus on emotion, not logic."* The AI responded: *"You weren't born to stare at clocks. Build a business that runs on your time."*

Miles grinned. That was it. Emotion. Identity. Freedom. He took the headline, wrote a heartfelt caption about his own story—how he'd once felt trapped in a cubicle—and ran the ad. Within days, engagement tripled. Comments poured in: *"This is exactly how I feel!"* and *"I needed to hear this today."* He wasn't just selling a course anymore; he was selling hope.

Encouraged, Miles dove deeper into psychology. He tested curiosity hooks like "The 3 words that doubled my sales overnight." He played with empowerment lines such as "Take control of your income—your future self will thank you." He noticed something fascinating: when his ads reflected how people *felt* instead of what they *needed*, performance exploded. AI became his creative amplifier, producing dozens of variations that echoed human emotion with data-driven precision.

But the breakthrough came with one ad—a campaign for a debt-relief app. The first drafts focused on features: "Lower your monthly payments with our smart algorithm." Results were mediocre. Then he changed the prompt: *"Write like you're talking to someone who's tired of being afraid to check their bank balance."* The output stunned him: *"You've spent enough nights worrying about bills. It's time to breathe again."*

That line hit him in the chest. It was real. Human. Vulnerable. He ran the ad, and it became his most successful campaign ever. Thousands clicked. Many sent messages thanking him for "finally understanding how it feels." That's when he realized AI could write emotion—but only if the human guiding it *felt* emotion too.

Miles started teaching this approach to his small agency team. He told them, "Our job isn't to sell products—it's to write what people wish someone would say to them." Together, they trained their AI assistant on emotion-based prompts. The machine learned to mimic empathy, curiosity, and encouragement. Their clients noticed the difference immediately. One eCommerce brand tripled conversions by changing "Shop now for great deals" to "You deserve to love what you wear again."

Late one night, as Miles scrolled through his campaigns, he saw the bigger picture. He wasn't just mastering AI tools—he was mastering human understanding. The screen showed numbers, but behind every click was a person feeling something: hope, relief, pride, curiosity. He leaned back and whispered, "This is what real marketing feels like."

A few weeks later, Miles was invited to speak at a digital marketing summit. He stood on stage and said, "AI can generate a thousand headlines in a minute. But only you can decide which one touches a heart." The audience nodded in silence, the weight of the truth settling in. AI might have changed the *process* of writing ads, but it hadn't changed the *purpose*. That purpose—to connect, inspire, and move—was eternal.

That night, Miles walked home feeling lighter. He realized that every ad he wrote from now on wasn't just about selling—it was about understanding. Behind every click, there was a story waiting to be told. And AI, when guided with empathy, was simply the pen that helped him tell it.

# Chapter 3: Crafting the Perfect Hook (Capturing Attention in Three Seconds)

Attention is the most expensive currency in marketing. In a world where billions of ads compete for a fraction of a second on a scrolling screen, your opening line—the *hook*—determines everything. Before the viewer decides to read, watch, or click, they must first decide to *stop*. That single moment of interruption is the copywriter's battlefield. A great hook doesn't just introduce; it seduces. It pulls the reader from passive scrolling into active curiosity. And in the AI era, crafting the perfect hook has become both an art and a science.

A hook works because it triggers instinctive human responses. Curiosity, surprise, self-interest, and relevance—these four emotions drive attention faster than logic ever could. Neurologically, a strong hook activates the brain's "seeking system," releasing dopamine and creating a need to resolve tension. That's why phrases like "Most people don't know this secret..." or "The truth nobody told you about..." still dominate social feeds. They open loops the human brain desperately wants to close. When used ethically, this principle can be one of the most powerful tools in your marketing arsenal.

AI can help you generate hundreds of hooks in seconds—but it's your understanding of *psychological triggers* that turns those hooks into gold. The secret is learning to write *pattern interrupts.* Humans are wired to ignore the familiar and notice the unusual. So, when everyone says "Buy now," your job is to say, "Wait—don't buy this yet." When most ads shout benefits, yours might whisper empathy: "I know what it's like to feel invisible." By prompting AI with instructions like "Create a pattern-interrupting hook that starts with curiosity and ends with emotional tension," you give it direction to break monotony.

Let's look at the anatomy of an effective hook. It contains four invisible forces: **Emotion, Contrast, Curiosity, and Benefit.** Emotion makes the reader *feel.* Contrast highlights something unexpected. Curiosity creates the desire to know more. Benefit answers "what's in it for me." For example: "You're losing sales every day—and you don't even know it." This line sparks emotion (fear of loss), contrast (hidden problem), curiosity (why?), and benefit (discovering the solution). AI tools can easily learn these elements by analyzing top-performing ads and combining emotional and logical cues within your prompts.

Another structure for effective hooks is the **You vs. Them** dynamic. People are drawn to identity-based storytelling. Hooks like "Most business owners will waste half their ad budget this year—don't be one of them" tap into competitiveness and belonging simultaneously. To generate these with AI, use prompts that include audience identifiers: *"Write a hook for freelancers who feel undervalued, highlighting the difference between average and elite."* You'll get results that emotionally connect to the reader's identity.

Then there's the **transformational hook**, which hints at a life or mindset change. "You don't need more followers—you need better buyers." "This one sentence made my ads 3x more profitable." These hooks promise improvement without revealing the full answer, compelling readers to continue. In your AI prompt, you might write: *"Generate transformation-based ad hooks that reframe a common belief."* This triggers contrast-driven curiosity, one of the strongest motivators in copywriting.

When crafting hooks with AI, always consider the **platform context.** What works on Facebook may fail on TikTok, and what grabs on YouTube might underperform on Instagram. AI can adapt tone and structure based on platform dynamics when guided correctly. For instance, a Facebook hook might be conversational and story-based ("I didn't believe this would work until I tried it myself..."), while a TikTok hook should be punchy, short, and emotion-first ("This ad almost got me fired—but it worked."). Include this context in your prompt to make AI platform-aware.

Don't overlook the **voice of authenticity.** The best hooks sound human, not robotic. Audiences crave connection. They want to feel spoken *to*, not sold *at*. That's why even AI-generated hooks need emotional calibration. After AI generates options, read them aloud. Do they sound natural? Would you actually say that to someone you care about? The subtle difference between "Discover how to boost sales instantly" and "Want to sell more without sounding salesy?" is what makes one line scroll-stopping and the other forgettable.

Finally, use **testing as your teacher.** Every audience is unique, and even the most persuasive hook is just a hypothesis until proven. AI allows you to create 20 variations of a headline, test each for engagement metrics, and refine based on results. Over time, patterns emerge—specific emotional tones, word lengths, or contrasts that consistently perform best for your brand. You can then train AI on those winning patterns to produce future hooks that mirror your top performers.

In the age of information overload, attention is power. AI gives you the ability to test faster, learn quicker, and write smarter. But the heart of every great hook still lies in empathy—the desire to make someone *feel something* in the first few seconds. Whether it's curiosity, hope, or shock, your goal is to make them stop scrolling long enough to think, "This one's for me." That's the moment you win.

*How Ava Got Her Three Seconds*

Ava sat in a crowded café, her laptop glowing with a half-finished ad campaign. Steam from her coffee curled beside the keyboard, a quiet reminder that time was slipping by. She was working on a client project for a fitness brand, and everything looked good on paper—catchy phrases, beautiful images, clear calls to action. Yet every time she ran the ads, the same story repeated: low clicks, low conversions, high frustration. She had mastered the technical side of advertising, but people weren't stopping long enough to read.

That night, scrolling through her own feed, Ava noticed something. She stopped at an ad that read, *"I used to cry in fitting rooms. Here's what changed."* It wasn't flashy, it wasn't loud—it was human. She clicked. It led to a powerful story about body confidence and transformation. The product—a simple home workout program—was almost secondary. But the hook? It spoke directly to emotion. Ava smiled. That's what she was missing. Not features. Not polish. Humanity.

Determined, she opened ChatGPT and wrote: *"Generate 10 emotional hooks for a fitness brand that focuses on self-confidence and empowerment, not weight loss."* Within seconds, the screen filled with lines like: "Strong looks different on everyone." "You don't need the perfect body to feel powerful." "This isn't about losing pounds—it's about gaining yourself." She felt a surge of excitement. These weren't just hooks—they were truths. She selected a few, built new ads around them, and launched them the next morning.

By the end of the week, her metrics told the story: engagement up 300%, comments full of personal stories, and a flood of messages from women saying the ad "spoke to their soul." The transformation wasn't just in her numbers—it was in her understanding. AI hadn't made her a better copywriter by giving her words; it had made her better by forcing her to understand *why* those words mattered.

But one ad in particular changed everything. The headline read, *"I stopped chasing perfection the day I started chasing peace."* The client hesitated at first—too emotional, they said. Ava insisted. Within 48 hours, it became their best-performing campaign ever. People didn't just click—they shared. They saved it. They commented things like, "This made me cry," and "Finally, an ad that gets it."

Later that night, Ava watched the campaign results roll in, the graphs climbing higher than any she'd seen before. It wasn't luck—it was connection. She realized she hadn't created an ad;

she'd created a mirror. A moment of reflection for the audience. And the spark that ignited it all was a single sentence—a hook.

Months later, when she began mentoring new marketers, she told them, "The first three seconds decide everything. You don't need to be loud—you need to be real." She taught them how to feed AI the right prompts, how to give it emotion and context, how to test dozens of hooks without losing their humanity. Her students were amazed that an algorithm could produce such heartfelt lines. But Ava reminded them, "It's not the AI that feels—it's *you*. The machine just amplifies your empathy."

Her reputation grew. Clients began calling her "the hook whisperer." She built a system that used AI to test emotional tones—hope, curiosity, nostalgia—and then adapt hooks based on the one that resonated most. Her ads didn't just sell; they started conversations. People felt seen, not targeted. And that, she realized, was the ultimate power of AI-assisted creativity: scaling authenticity.

One evening, as she walked home under the city lights, Ava thought back to that first ad that stopped her mid-scroll. "I used to cry in fitting rooms." She smiled, remembering how a single sentence changed the way she saw marketing forever. It wasn't about products. It wasn't even about profit. It was about presence—showing up in someone's feed and saying something that mattered. The hook wasn't the beginning of an ad; it was the beginning of a connection.

# Chapter 4: Mastering Emotional Tone (Writing Ads That Make People Feel)

If a hook captures attention, emotional tone keeps it. Great copy is more than clever phrasing—it's emotional architecture. It's the heartbeat of your message, the invisible energy that determines whether readers feel inspired, understood, or indifferent. Tone is what transforms generic words into powerful emotions, shaping not only *what* people read but *how* they experience it. AI tools can generate endless combinations of sentences, but unless those sentences carry feeling, they remain lifeless. Emotion is the difference between "Buy now" and "This could be the moment everything changes for you."

Every audience responds to emotion differently. Some are motivated by hope, others by fear, others by belonging or curiosity. The secret of emotional copywriting is alignment: matching the right emotion to the reader's current mindset. A first-time entrepreneur may respond to encouragement ("You can build something amazing from nothing"), while an experienced marketer might need excitement ("You're one funnel away from scaling beyond belief"). Emotional tone isn't about dramatics—it's about resonance. It's speaking the emotional language your audience already feels but hasn't yet articulated.

In AI copywriting, tone control begins with **intentional prompting**. You can direct an AI model to write in specific emotional styles—compassionate, confident, inspiring, humorous, or authoritative—by using explicit tone instructions. For example, "Write in an encouraging tone that feels like a mentor guiding a friend," or "Create urgency without pressure using a hopeful tone." The more emotional cues you embed in your prompt, the closer AI gets to the human rhythm of empathy. Over time, you can train your AI assistant to recognize your brand's emotional palette and replicate it consistently across ads, captions, and landing pages.

Understanding tone also means understanding **emotional progression.** Every effective ad takes the reader on a short emotional journey: from tension to relief, from doubt to confidence, from confusion to clarity. A well-structured tone arc follows the human decision path. For instance, you might start an ad with empathy ("You've tried everything, and nothing seems to work"), then move to hope ("But what if the answer wasn't working harder, but smarter?"), and end with empowerment ("AI copywriting gives you the clarity to win every campaign"). This three-step emotional rhythm keeps engagement high and naturally leads toward conversion.

Different emotional tones serve different purposes:

- **Empathy** builds trust. Use it to connect.
- **Excitement** drives action. Use it to motivate.
- **Authority** creates confidence. Use it to close.
- **Humor** disarms skepticism. Use it to humanize.
- **Inspiration** elevates perception. Use it to brand.

When crafting prompts, think like a director giving emotional direction to an actor. Instead of saying, "Write a Facebook ad for a course," you might say, "Write a Facebook ad that feels like a close friend cheering for your success after you've failed multiple times." The difference in tone is dramatic—and instantly more relatable.

AI tools can now measure *emotional valence*—the positive or negative energy of your words. You can analyze your copy's tone to ensure it aligns with your desired emotional target. For example, if an ad meant to inspire comes across as desperate, you can adjust word choice to restore balance. Replace "Don't miss your chance" (fear of loss) with "Your next big opportunity is waiting" (hope and anticipation). These subtle shifts redefine how the audience interprets your brand personality.

It's also essential to understand **cultural and contextual sensitivity**. What feels exciting in one market may feel aggressive in another. AI can adapt tone by region or audience type if guided properly. For instance, instructing AI to "write in a warm, family-oriented tone for Latin American audiences" will produce very different copy than "write in a minimalist, data-driven tone for tech executives." The best marketers master emotional translation—communicating the same idea in different emotional dialects.

Emotional tone determines how long your brand stays in someone's memory. People rarely remember facts, but they always remember feelings. That's why the most successful ads in history—Nike's "Just Do It," Apple's "Think Different," or Dove's "Real Beauty"—aren't just slogans; they're emotional philosophies. AI can now learn from those archetypes and apply similar tonal structures to your own campaigns. By studying emotional success patterns and combining them with your own authentic voice, you can scale human emotion across thousands of ad variations without losing heart.

In the end, tone isn't decoration—it's direction. It guides the reader's heart toward a decision. When you infuse emotion into your AI prompts, you create a language that feels personal even when automated. The future of advertising isn't just intelligent—it's empathetic. The brands that win will be the ones that make people feel something real.

### *Isabella Finally Mastered Emotional Ads*

Isabella stared at her laptop, reading the ad she'd written for the tenth time. It was perfect—at least technically. Every sentence was concise, every benefit clear. Yet something about it felt hollow. She knew the audience she was trying to reach—new entrepreneurs who'd burned out chasing leads—but the copy sounded like a machine selling hope. She sighed and closed her eyes. "I wouldn't click this," she whispered.

That night, she replayed a conversation she'd had years ago with her mentor. "Words only matter when they make people feel," he'd told her. She remembered laughing it off back then, confident that logic sold better than emotion. But now, as she watched ad after ad fail to connect, his words echoed louder than ever.

The next morning, she opened her AI copy assistant and typed: *"Write an ad for entrepreneurs who feel tired and unmotivated. Use a gentle, understanding tone. Sound like a friend who's been through it too."*

The AI responded: *"You don't need to hustle harder—you just need to breathe again. Build your business without losing yourself in the process."*

Isabella felt a chill. It was the first time an ad she'd read felt like a conversation instead of a command. She built a campaign around it, pairing the words with soft visuals and calm music. Within days, the results stunned her—comments like *"I felt this"* and *"This is exactly where I am right now."* The numbers followed—engagement up, cost per click down. But more than that, something had shifted in her understanding of marketing.

A week later, she met with her client, a small wellness coach who'd struggled to grow her brand. When Isabella showed her the results, the client's eyes filled with tears. "People finally get what I'm trying to say," she whispered. That moment hit Isabella harder than any data report. Emotion wasn't just a strategy; it was connection.

From that day forward, Isabella became obsessed with emotional tone. She experimented with different energies—humor, warmth, authority—and tested how each influenced perception. She discovered that empathy built trust faster than discounts, that curiosity sparked engagement longer than urgency, and that inspiration created loyalty where logic couldn't. AI became her emotional amplifier. She learned to program it not just with keywords but with feelings. Her prompts started sounding like stage directions: "Write this like a coach who believes in you," or "Sound like the voice in someone's head reminding them not to give up." One campaign changed her life. It was for a non-profit helping single mothers start small businesses. She asked AI to write in a "hopeful yet respectful" tone. The ad began with: *"You've carried everyone else's dreams long enough. Maybe it's time to build your own."* It spread like wildfire. Donations doubled, applications poured in, and mothers wrote to say the ad gave them courage. Isabella cried reading their messages. She'd found her purpose again—writing words that moved souls, not just statistics.

At a marketing summit months later, she presented her process to a packed room. "AI can analyze millions of emotions," she told them, "but it can't *care*. That's still your job." The crowd nodded, many jotting down her advice on "emotional prompting." She closed with one sentence: "Your audience doesn't want to be impressed—they want to be understood."

That evening, back in her apartment, Isabella opened her laptop to plan her next campaign. She smiled as she typed her first line to the AI: *"Let's write something that makes someone feel seen today."* It was simple, but it had become her mantra. The numbers mattered, of course—but now, they were secondary. What truly mattered was impact. She had rediscovered the heartbeat of marketing: emotion guided by empathy.

# Chapter 5: The Science of Headlines (Turning Curiosity Into Clicks)

If emotional tone makes people *feel*, headlines make them *act*. A headline is the first handshake between your message and your audience. It determines whether someone stops to read, scrolls past, or clicks to learn more. In digital advertising, the headline isn't merely a title—it's the engine of conversion. Studies show that 80% of people read headlines, but only 20% read the rest. That means your headline must do 80% of the work in a fraction of a second. The art of writing great headlines has always blended creativity, psychology, and precision—but now, with AI, you can add science to that mix.

AI copywriting tools analyze millions of successful ads across industries to detect which headline patterns perform best. They study structure, length, emotion, and even punctuation to identify what triggers engagement. This means you no longer need to guess whether "Unlock Your Potential" will outperform "Discover the Shortcut to Success." AI can provide data-backed predictions and generate headline variants optimized for click-through rate, engagement, and emotional impact. But for this to work, you must feed it strategic direction through thoughtful prompting.

A great headline follows one or more of the **four C's of**

**conversion: Clear, Concise, Compelling, and Credible.**

- **Clear:** It communicates the offer or idea immediately.
- **Concise:** It respects attention spans by using few words powerfully.
- **Compelling:** It sparks emotion or curiosity.
- **Credible:** It feels trustworthy and real.

For instance, "Learn to Write Ads That Sell" is clear and concise but lacks intrigue. Add curiosity, and it becomes "The Ad Writing Method That Makes People Buy Without Selling." That extra detail transforms information into fascination. AI can instantly generate variations like these when prompted to balance clarity with curiosity.

When crafting AI prompts for headlines, start with *intent*. Do you want to inspire, educate, or provoke? Example prompt: *"Generate 10 Facebook ad headlines that use curiosity and transformation to promote a course on AI copywriting."* The results might include:

- "Write Less. Sell More. Let AI Do the Heavy Lifting."
- "The Hidden Formula Behind Every 7-Figure Ad Copy."
- "One Prompt Can Change Your Marketing Forever."

You'll notice that each variation has a different emotional pull—efficiency, intrigue, or empowerment. You can then test these themes to see which connects most strongly with your audience.

There are also time-tested headline formulas that work across niches, many of which can be taught to AI:

1. **How-to Headlines** – "How to [Achieve X] Without [Pain Y]"
   - Example: "How to Write Profitable Ads Without Spending Hours Brainstorming."
2. **Question Headlines** – "Are You Making This Mistake?"
   - Example: "Are You Letting Your Ads Sound Like Everyone Else's?"
3. **Result Headlines** – "Get [Result] in [Time] Using [Method]."
   - Example: "Get 5X Engagement in a Week Using Smart AI Prompts."
4. **Secret or Insider Headlines** – "The Secret Every Top Marketer Knows."

    - Example: "The Hidden Trick AI Copywriters Use to Double Click-Through Rates."

5. **Emotional Benefit Headlines** – "Stop [Pain] and Start [Desire]."

    - Example: "Stop Guessing What Works. Start Selling With Confidence."

When AI generates headlines, it's easy to fall into repetition—many will sound similar or cliché. The secret is *layering context.* Add details about your audience, tone, or outcome. For instance: *"Write 10 headlines for busy solopreneurs who want to use AI to save time and grow their business."* This will produce results that resonate deeper because they're emotionally targeted.

Testing remains your greatest advantage. With AI, you can A/B test dozens of headlines simultaneously, measuring which tone (urgent vs. hopeful), structure (question vs. statement), or focus (benefit vs. fear) performs best. Over time, you'll develop your own *headline DNA*—a pattern of emotional triggers and phrasing styles that consistently outperform.

But data alone doesn't win hearts. The most viral headlines often contain an element of truth that feels *personal.* "You Don't Need More Followers—You Need Better Clients." "You're

One Skill Away From Changing Your Future." These lines feel like advice from a trusted friend, not a brand. The goal is to humanize the data—make it sound like one human speaking to another.

In the end, headline mastery is the balance between formula and feeling, logic and emotion, data and intuition. AI provides the structure, but your empathy gives it meaning. The best headlines make people pause—not because they're shocking, but because they sound like something they've been waiting to hear. That's the real power of modern AI copywriting: words that feel algorithmically smart and emotionally human.

### *Jason Decides to Let AI Write 20 Headlines*

Jared's office was filled with the quiet hum of computers and the faint buzz of city noise through the window. He worked as a digital marketing strategist for a mid-sized eCommerce brand, and lately, the numbers were keeping him up at night. Ad costs were rising, conversions were dropping, and despite using every tool imaginable, his campaigns were losing their spark. "The product's great," his manager had said. "We just need people to notice it." But no one was noticing.

He sat at his desk late one evening, staring at rows of performance data. Every metric screamed the same truth—people weren't clicking. His headlines were too safe, too predictable. "Shop the New Collection." "Discover the Sale Everyone's Talking About." It all sounded like static. Out of frustration, he turned to his AI writing assistant and typed: *"Write me 20 headlines that sound nothing like traditional ads."*

Seconds later, the screen filled with ideas:

- "You Don't Need New Clothes. You Need a New Mood."
- "This Isn't Fashion. It's a Reminder You're Alive."
- "Try Not to Fall in Love With These."

Jared laughed out loud. "Now *that*," he thought, "feels alive." He tested the headlines. Within 48 hours, click-through rates doubled. One line—*"You Don't Need New Clothes. You Need a New Mood."*—outperformed every other by a mile. It wasn't just catchy; it made people *feel*. Comments poured in. People tagged friends. The brand's tone suddenly shifted from generic to soulful.

Encouraged, Jared started diving deeper. He read books on advertising psychology and noticed a pattern—every iconic headline from history sparked curiosity or emotion. "Think Small." "Because You're Worth It." "The Ultimate Driving Machine." These weren't about features. They were about *identity*. He realized that a headline wasn't a summary—it was a mirror reflecting the reader's inner thoughts.

He started using AI differently. Instead of asking it to "write headlines," he prompted it with emotion: *"Write headlines that make people curious about freedom."* or *"Write headlines that sound like hope disguised as marketing."* The results stunned him. Each one felt like it had a pulse. "Escape the Noise. Find Your Own Rhythm." "You Don't Need Permission to Start Over." The data confirmed what his gut already knew—emotion outperformed information.

One campaign changed everything. The brand launched a mental health awareness collection, and Jared wrote the headline: *"Wear the Reminder You're Still Healing."* The team hesitated. "Isn't that too heavy?" someone asked. Jared shook his head. "It's honest." When the campaign went live, it went viral. Thousands shared the post, thanking the brand for being *real.* Sales skyrocketed, but what meant most were the comments—people saying they felt seen.

Weeks later, at a creative retreat, a young marketer asked Jared, "What's the secret to a perfect headline?" He smiled. "It's not about being clever," he said. "It's about making someone stop and whisper, 'That's me.'" He explained how AI could write a hundred lines in seconds, but only a human could decide which one carried truth. "AI gives you the words," he said, "but *you* give them meaning." That night, back in his apartment, Jared sat with his laptop and wrote himself a reminder: *"A headline is a bridge between noise and understanding."* He looked out at the city lights and thought about how much marketing had changed—and yet, how little had. In every era, in every platform, people just wanted to feel connected. The tools had evolved, but the goal remained timeless. He smiled as he opened a new project and typed his first prompt: *"Let's write something that makes people curious enough to care."*

# Chapter 6: AI Ad Prompts That Sell (Speaking the Language of Persuasion)

If words are the weapon, prompts are the trigger. In the world of AI copywriting, your results are only as strong as your instructions. The prompt you give determines the structure, tone, emotion, and outcome of every ad. Think of AI as the most brilliant intern you've ever hired—capable of incredible creativity, but only when guided clearly. The more specific, emotionally intelligent, and strategic your prompts are, the more human and persuasive the output becomes. Mastering prompts is like mastering the new language of marketing—one where psychology, data, and emotion combine into one line of direction.

A good AI prompt begins with **clarity of purpose.** Before writing, ask yourself: What is the goal of this ad? Are you trying to build awareness, drive clicks, or close a sale? Each goal demands a different tone. For example, if your goal is brand awareness, you might prompt, "Write a short, inspiring Facebook ad introducing an AI copywriting course that helps creators find their voice." For direct sales, the prompt could shift to: "Write a persuasive ad that sells an AI copywriting course by emphasizing transformation and guaranteed results." One word—"introducing" versus "selling"—changes the entire energy of the copy.

Next comes **context.** AI performs best when it understands your audience deeply. Adding demographic, emotional, and situational details makes your prompts exponentially more powerful. For instance: "Write a LinkedIn ad for overworked entrepreneurs who struggle with writing consistent marketing content. Use an encouraging and time-saving tone." Compare that to: "Write an ad for business owners." The second is generic; the first speaks directly to pain points. AI needs empathy to produce persuasion—and you create that empathy through detailed prompting.

Effective prompts also include **emotional direction.** You can't expect emotion from an AI unless you tell it what emotion to channel. You might say: "Write in a hopeful and motivating tone," "Use empathetic storytelling that builds trust," or "Inspire curiosity and wonder in the first sentence." These cues help AI shape rhythm, sentence structure, and pacing in ways that feel alive. Just like a film director gives emotional cues to actors, you give emotional direction to the AI to ensure your copy connects rather than sounds robotic.

One of the most powerful ways to use AI for persuasion is through **framework prompting.** Classic copywriting formulas—AIDA (Attention, Interest, Desire, Action), PAS

(Problem, Agitation, Solution), and FAB (Features, Advantages, Benefits)—can be integrated into your instructions. For example: “Write a PAS-style Instagram ad for a fitness app that helps busy parents get in shape without gym memberships.” The AI will structure the copy with empathy for the problem, emotional amplification, and a satisfying solution. By naming the formula, you give the AI creative boundaries within which it can shine.

Equally important is **tone replication.** AI can mimic brand voices when trained on sample text. If you feed it previous ads, emails, or captions, you can prompt: “Write in the same tone as this example—professional yet conversational, confident but not arrogant.” Over time, this builds consistency across campaigns. Tone training transforms AI from a tool into a brand ally, allowing your copy to sound like “you” every time, even when written by a machine.

Another overlooked tactic is using **multi-step prompting.** Instead of asking AI for the final copy immediately, you can break the process into stages:

1. Generate 10 headlines.
2. Pick the most emotional and attention-grabbing ones.
3. Write 3 ad versions for each.

4. Add calls to action that sound conversational and confident.

This step-by-step structure mirrors how professional writers think—drafting, revising, testing, and refining—and helps AI build depth and logic in its outputs.

When writing prompts for high-performing ads, always include **constraints** that ensure realism and focus. For instance, specify platform length limits ("Write a 150-character Instagram caption" or "Write a two-sentence TikTok ad hook") or creative context ("Include a question and end with an emotional call to action"). Constraints force precision, turning long-winded AI output into crisp, punchy marketing.

As you master prompting, you'll begin to see patterns emerge—certain words or emotional setups that consistently lead to better results. These are your *signature triggers*. You might find that prompts using "imagine," "finally," or "without stress" generate more engagement because they blend emotion with relief. Once you identify them, you can save them as reusable templates and train your AI to start with those structures.

AI prompting isn't just technical—it's psychological communication. You're not instructing a computer; you're coaching a mirror of collective human language. The more emotion, intent, and structure you give it, the more it gives back. Every masterpiece of modern marketing begins not with a blank screen, but with one great line of direction. Learn to master that, and you'll never fear a blinking cursor again.

### *Now Noah Speaks the Language of Persuasion*

Noah stared at his empty Google Doc, fingers frozen above the keyboard. He'd spent years as a marketing consultant, but lately, his clients wanted something different—faster results, higher engagement, less guesswork. "Can't AI just write the ads for us?" one client had asked. Noah had laughed, but deep down, he wondered if it was possible. That night, curiosity won. He opened his AI writing tool and typed his first hesitant command: *"Write an ad that sells an online course about productivity."*

The AI replied instantly with a neat paragraph full of buzzwords: "Unlock your potential. Boost your productivity. Achieve success." Noah frowned. It was clean, but soulless—like a corporate memo wearing perfume. He deleted it and leaned back, thinking. "Maybe it's not the AI that's bad," he murmured. "Maybe it's me. Maybe I'm not asking the right question."

He tried again: *"Write a short Facebook ad for busy entrepreneurs who feel burned out and want a system to regain focus. Sound like a mentor who's been there."*

This time, the words came alive: *"You don't need more hours in the day—you need a smarter way to use them. I used to drown in deadlines until I learned how to automate focus. Here's how you can too."*

Noah's eyes widened. The tone was warm, personal, almost human. It didn't feel like a machine anymore—it felt like a conversation. He tested the ad. Within two days, it outperformed every other campaign he'd written in months. The secret, he realized, wasn't the AI—it was the prompt. The better he spoke to it, the better it spoke back.

He started experimenting. He told the AI to write like a coach, a friend, a storyteller. Each time, the copy shifted completely, adapting tone and rhythm as if it understood him. "This thing doesn't need direction," he said one night, grinning. "It needs leadership." He began treating prompts like creative briefs—complete with audience profiles, emotional cues, and frameworks. "Write a PAS-style ad for solopreneurs who want freedom from burnout," he typed one evening. The result? A masterpiece that made readers feel seen, not sold to.

The transformation didn't stop at his own work. Noah began teaching his clients how to "talk to AI." In workshops, he'd say, "You don't get what you *ask* for—you get what you *communicate.*" He showed them how to add empathy to their instructions, how to layer emotional direction, how to describe the reader's state of mind. One client—a real estate agent struggling with stale ads—followed Noah's approach and saw her engagement triple in a week. Her secret? A simple prompt: *"Write like you're talking to someone who's scared to take the first step toward owning a home."*

Noah's reputation grew. Soon, companies were hiring him not to write ads, but to train their teams on AI prompting. "You're like a language translator," one CEO told him. "You teach people how to speak 'machine empathy.'" He laughed, but the phrase stuck. That's exactly what it was—empathy through algorithms. The better humans understood emotion, the more powerfully AI could communicate it.

One night, Noah sat on his balcony overlooking the city, thinking about how far things had come. The world had changed. Marketers once obsessed over keywords and algorithms; now they were learning to blend emotion with instruction. He sipped his coffee and whispered to himself, "The future belongs to those who know how to ask."

Before closing his laptop, he typed one last reminder into his notes: *"Don't fear AI. Teach it to feel."*

It became the mantra of his workshops. He would tell his students, "AI doesn't replace creativity—it responds to it. Your prompt is your philosophy in disguise. If you write it with empathy, your ads will sell themselves." And as he watched a new generation of marketers find their rhythm, he smiled, knowing that the language of persuasion had evolved—but its heart had stayed the same.

# Chapter 7: The Brand Voice Blueprint (Teaching AI to Sound Like You)

Every great brand has a voice. It's the personality behind the words, the emotional fingerprint that separates a message from the noise. Coca-Cola sounds joyful. Apple sounds visionary. Nike sounds daring. These brands don't just sell products—they sell identity, and that identity lives in their tone of voice. In the age of AI copywriting, brand voice has become both a creative asset and a technical necessity. Without it, your ads may sound competent but anonymous. With it, every headline, caption, and story you publish feels unmistakably *you*.

The goal of this chapter is to help you teach AI how to replicate your brand voice with precision, emotion, and authenticity. This process is called **voice modeling**, and it's one of the most powerful ways to humanize AI-generated content. When done right, it ensures that every ad you publish sounds cohesive, familiar, and emotionally consistent—whether written by you, your team, or your AI assistant.

The first step in defining brand voice is **self-awareness.** Ask yourself: What do I want my brand to make people feel? Trust? Energy? Belonging? Inspiration? These emotional anchors guide tone choices in your copy. For example, a wellness brand might want to sound nurturing and calm, while a fintech company might prefer confidence and authority. Write a one-sentence mission statement describing your voice: "We speak like a mentor guiding a friend toward freedom," or "We sound like innovation made simple." This becomes the emotional core of your voice.

Next, analyze your **existing content.** Collect a few examples of your best-performing posts, ads, or emails. Read them aloud and identify patterns in language. Do you use contractions ("you're," "we're") or formal phrasing? Do you favor optimism ("you can do this") or realism ("here's what it really takes")? AI learns patterns—so the clearer you define them, the more accurately it can mirror your style. Once identified, list your three key tone descriptors. For example: *Encouraging. Clear. Empowering.*

Now you can create a **voice prompt framework**—a structured way to "train" AI every time you write. For example:

> "Write a Facebook ad in an encouraging, conversational tone. Use simple, human language that feels confident but warm. Avoid exaggeration or aggressive sales language."

This framework ensures every AI-generated piece stays on-brand, no matter the topic. Over time, you can build a voice library—templates, catchphrases, and tonal examples—that your AI references automatically.

Another critical concept is **emotional consistency.** Your tone should evolve slightly across platforms without losing its identity. On LinkedIn, you might sound professional and reflective. On Instagram, more playful and direct. On YouTube, conversational and authentic. The emotional core stays the same, but the surface adjusts. You can train AI for this by adding platform context to your prompts:

> "Write this in our brand's empowering tone, but adapt it for Instagram Reels—keep it shorter, more emotional, and use rhythm and punch."

AI can even help you maintain *brand memory.* By feeding it past examples of your copy and instructing, "Match this tone and structure," it can recall rhythm, pacing, and energy unique to your style. Many advanced users now fine-tune models using their personal brand archives, allowing the AI to internalize everything from sentence cadence to emotional color.

But a powerful voice is about more than tone—it's about **values.** People connect to brands that sound human because humans stand for something. Clarify your principles. For example: "We always empower, never pressure." "We educate before we sell." "We speak hope, not fear." By embedding these into your prompts—"Write this ad using our brand value of empowerment"—you create consistency that transcends words.

One final and overlooked element of brand voice is **story rhythm.** Every brand tells its story differently. Some use transformation arcs ("I used to struggle until..."), others use insight ("Most people don't realize that..."). Teach AI which structure aligns with your personality. This keeps your storytelling natural and recognizable, even when scaled through automation.

When your AI truly understands your voice, you'll notice a shift: your ads start feeling alive again. Readers will say things like, "I knew this was your post before I even saw your logo." That's the magic of brand identity—a feeling of continuity that makes your message unforgettable. AI can handle the automation, but you supply the soul.

The future of advertising will belong to creators and brands that sound real, familiar, and emotionally magnetic. When you combine authenticity with AI precision, you create something powerful: a voice that can scale infinitely without losing its humanity.

*Sophie's Clients Wanted Unique Voices*

Sophie leaned back in her chair, exhausted. Her marketing agency had grown fast—too fast. Between managing clients, social media, and ads, she'd started relying heavily on AI tools to generate copy. At first, it was amazing. Deadlines vanished overnight. Content poured out faster than ever. But over time, she noticed something unsettling. All her ads started sounding... the same. Different brands, same rhythm. Different industries, same voice. Clean, polished, and utterly forgettable.

One night, she opened her inbox to find an email from a longtime client. *"We love the results,"* it said, *"but it doesn't sound like us anymore."* The words hit her harder than she expected. She realized she'd lost the very thing that had built her business in the first place—her clients' unique voices.

Determined to fix it, Sophie spent the next morning studying her favorite brands. She analyzed Nike's bold tone, Apple's elegant simplicity, and Airbnb's feeling of belonging. Each had a heartbeat in their words. Their copy didn't sound written—it sounded *alive*. That's when it clicked. AI could generate words, but only humans could define voice.

She opened her AI assistant and wrote a different kind of prompt: *"Write an ad for a skincare brand that sounds soft, reassuring, and wise—like an older sister sharing advice, not a company making a pitch."*

The output stunned her. It began: *"Your skin doesn't need perfection—it needs patience. Start with kindness, and everything else follows."*

Tears welled in her eyes. It was simple. Human. Real. The kind of line that felt like truth, not marketing. She shared it with her client, who immediately replied: *"This is us. This is exactly our voice."*

Encouraged, Sophie began developing what she called *The Voice Blueprint*. She asked every client a few deep questions: "If your brand were a person, how would they speak?" "What emotion do you want people to feel after reading your words?" "What values guide your tone?" She turned their answers into prompts like: *"Write in a hopeful, empowering voice that sounds like a mentor guiding someone toward freedom."*

Soon, her campaigns transformed. A real estate client's ads began sounding trustworthy and confident. A wellness coach's posts radiated peace. A tech startup's content felt visionary but human. Engagement soared, but what meant more were the comments—people saying, *"This feels real," "I love your energy,"* or *"You always say what I'm thinking."*

Then came the day that changed everything. Sophie received an inquiry from a major brand asking if she could "train their AI" to speak in their exact tone. It was a massive project. She gathered their past campaigns, analyzed their most successful ads, and created a prompt library defining everything from their rhythm to their emotional range. When the first AI-generated drafts came back, the marketing director was speechless. "It sounds like us," he whispered. "It even *feels* like us."

From that moment on, Sophie's agency shifted direction. She stopped calling herself a copywriter. She became a *voice architect*. Her job wasn't just to write—it was to translate emotion into instruction, to teach machines how to carry human identity. She trained dozens of assistants to replicate unique brand voices, from humorous to soulful, from authoritative to poetic. Her secret was simple: every great prompt began with empathy.

Months later, as Sophie sat at her desk late one night, reviewing the week's campaigns, she noticed something beautiful. Each brand sounded distinct again—alive, expressive, and real. She smiled, remembering her old fear that AI would make everything sound robotic. Now she knew the truth. AI didn't erase voice—it amplified it, as long as you led with humanity.

She closed her laptop and wrote one line on her notepad before turning off the lights: *"Voice isn't what you say. It's how you make people feel when you say it."*

That single sentence became her company's slogan—and the compass that guided every word she and her AI partners ever wrote again.

# Chapter 8: Visual Triggers in Words (Writing Copy That People See and Feel)

A picture may be worth a thousand words—but the right words can *create* a thousand pictures. In advertising, great copy doesn't just tell; it *shows*. It paints vivid mental images that make the reader feel like they're already living the transformation being promised. This is what's called *visual copywriting*: using language so descriptive, emotional, and sensory that the brain interprets it like an image. When paired with AI tools that understand tone, metaphor, and rhythm, visual writing becomes a force that pulls readers into your story before they even see the ad image.

Humans process visuals 60,000 times faster than text, but the subconscious can't tell the difference between a vividly imagined scene and a real one. That's why visual copy activates emotional response instantly. Words like *"imagine," "picture this," "feel the difference,"* or *"see yourself"* trigger visualization and emotional engagement. The best AI copywriters leverage this psychology through prompts that direct the model to use sensory, emotional, and narrative cues. For example:

> "Write an ad that helps the reader imagine waking up debt-free for the first time in years—focus on

relief, calm, and freedom." AI will generate text that sounds cinematic: "You open your eyes to quiet. No more dread. Just peace—and the freedom to start again." The words themselves create imagery, emotion, and motion.

To master this style, combine **storytelling + sensory details + transformation.** A simple structure looks like this:

1. *Open with visualization* – "Imagine walking into your dream home..."

2. *Add emotion* – "...the one you thought you'd never afford."

3. *Present the transformation* – "Now, AI-powered mortgage tools make it possible." Each line builds on the previous, creating a visual story that invites readers to participate emotionally.

You can guide AI to write visually by including prompts like: "Use descriptive language that appeals to the senses," or "Write copy that feels cinematic, showing emotion through imagery." These cues help AI switch from abstract marketing language to storytelling language. Instead of "Boost your income," you'll get "Watch your bank account grow while your stress fades." One *tells* the benefit; the other *shows* it.

Visual writing also strengthens **brand association.** People remember feelings linked to images. When your copy consistently evokes visual emotion—freedom, relief, luxury, growth—it trains the audience to associate those emotions with your brand identity. AI tools can be trained to reproduce these emotional visuals by analyzing your most successful campaigns. Prompt it to "write in the tone and imagery style of this ad," and the model will mimic pacing, energy, and sensory depth.

Another key is **metaphorical persuasion.** Metaphors translate complex ideas into instantly understandable pictures. "Your credit score is the key to your financial future." "AI is your silent copywriting partner." "Your business deserves a louder microphone." These phrases make intangible concepts tangible. You can prompt AI specifically for metaphor-based copy: "Use a visual metaphor to explain how AI helps small businesses grow." The model might respond with something like: "Think of AI as your marketing compass—it guides you toward profit with every decision." Metaphors connect intellect to instinct, making ads unforgettable.

To create stronger mental pictures, mix sensory words:

- **Sight:** bright, clear, golden, shimmering
- **Sound:** whisper, hum, roar, echo
- **Touch:** smooth, cold, warm, electric
- **Taste/Smell:** crisp, smoky, sweet, refreshing AI understands these associations and can use them strategically when you prompt it to "add sensory emotion." It's one of the fastest ways to make digital words feel human again.

Finally, combine *visual copywriting* with *AI testing*. Run variations that use different imagery styles—one focusing on freedom, one on confidence, one on security—and analyze which resonates most with your audience. Over time, you'll develop a "visual tone map" for your brand, showing which emotional pictures drive the highest engagement and conversion.

In essence, the future of copywriting is hybrid: half data, half imagination. AI provides the logic; you provide the color. Together, they create marketing that doesn't just speak to the eyes—but to the heart.

### *Numbers Are for Clara but...*

Clara was known for being a numbers-driven marketer. She loved spreadsheets, analytics, and clean data visualizations. Her ads performed decently, but she often felt something was missing—a sense of connection, an emotional spark. One afternoon, while reviewing campaign reports for a travel brand, she noticed something strange: the ad with the worst data headline had the *best* click-through rate. Its headline? *"Smell the ocean before you even pack your bags."*

She clicked through the ad and read the copy. It didn't sell; it *transported.* "Feel the sand between your toes. Hear the waves crash outside your window. This isn't a vacation—it's your story waiting to be written." Clara realized that the ad wasn't describing a product; it was describing an experience. That night, she decided to learn the art of *visual copywriting*.

The next morning, she opened her AI assistant and typed: *"Write an ad for a coffee brand that makes the reader taste and smell the morning before they've even brewed it."*

Within seconds, the words appeared: *"The first sip isn't coffee—it's sunrise. The warmth against your palms, the quiet promise of a new day. Start it with flavor that feels alive."*

Clara sat back, speechless. It was poetic, but not pretentious. Emotional, but grounded. She ran the ad—and it became the highest-performing post the brand had ever seen. Customers commented things like, *"I could smell this ad!"* and *"I felt the warmth just reading it."*

Encouraged, Clara began rewriting all her campaigns with one new rule: "If they can't *see* it, they won't *feel* it." She used prompts that instructed AI to "paint a picture with words." Her financial client's ads changed from "Achieve financial freedom" to "Imagine logging into your account and smiling for the first time." Her fitness brand campaigns stopped saying "Lose weight fast" and started saying "Watch your reflection change before your mindset does."

Then came her biggest challenge—a car company known for dry, feature-heavy ads. The client demanded something different, something emotional. Clara smiled. She knew exactly what to do. Her prompt read: *"Write an ad that lets the reader feel the thrill of driving before they even touch the wheel. Use motion, sound, and light."* The AI generated: *"The road hums beneath you. The horizon opens like a secret. Every curve, every whisper of wind, feels like freedom."*

The client was stunned. "This doesn't sound like an ad," he said. "It sounds like a movie." Clara grinned. "Exactly." The campaign went viral. People weren't just seeing cars—they were *feeling* the journey.

Months later, Clara spoke at a creative conference. On stage, she told the story of how she stopped writing ads and started directing emotions. "AI can calculate," she said, "but you can teach it to *imagine*. When you write, don't describe the product. Describe the *moment*."

After her talk, a young marketer approached her. "How do you know when your copy is visual enough?" he asked. Clara smiled. "When you close your eyes," she said, "and the words still play like a movie."

That night, she returned to her office and stared at a blank screen. The cursor blinked like an invitation. She whispered to herself, "Let's make them see it." Then she began typing, weaving words into images, images into emotion, and emotion into action. From that moment forward, her ads didn't just convert—they *moved* people.

# Chapter 9: Conversion Architecture (Structuring AI Ads That Sell Themselves)

Every successful ad follows a structure—a rhythm of emotion and logic that moves the reader from curiosity to commitment. This isn't luck or coincidence; it's conversion architecture. It's the deliberate sequencing of ideas, emotions, and proof that turn attention into trust and trust into action. The most effective marketers don't just write copy—they design experiences. Each sentence, image, and call-to-action (CTA) is placed with psychological precision. In the age of AI, you can now engineer these structures faster than ever, using prompts that replicate the science of persuasion with machine-level consistency and human-level heart.

The first pillar of conversion architecture is **The Hook.** You already know the importance of capturing attention, but in structural terms, it's your entry point—the first emotional handshake. It must stop the scroll, introduce tension, and signal value. For example: "You don't need more followers—you need better buyers." A great prompt might be: *"Write a hook that challenges a common belief in a confident but relatable tone."* AI will then create a line that instantly reframes the reader's perspective, setting up curiosity for what comes next.

The second pillar is **The Story.** Humans remember stories, not facts. After your hook, you need a bridge—a relatable scenario or emotional image that grounds your message. This section answers the reader's unspoken question: "Why should I care?" In AI prompting, you can guide this phase with: *"Add a short, emotionally relatable story that mirrors the reader's struggle before revealing the solution."* This gives your ad depth, humanity, and flow.

Next comes **The Solution.** This is where clarity meets transformation. You present your offer, your system, or your product as the answer to the problem raised earlier. Avoid vague promises. Use AI to generate concrete benefits framed through emotion. For example, instead of "AI tools make marketing easier," try "With AI, you'll spend less time guessing and more time winning." You can direct AI to use the "Problem → Agitation → Solution" (PAS) framework to ensure your message hits both pain and relief points.

The fourth element is **Proof.** This is where trust solidifies. Without proof, even the best story feels incomplete. Testimonials, data, screenshots, or case studies make the emotional argument credible. You can prompt AI with instructions like: *"Add one line of social proof or credibility that reinforces trust without sounding salesy."* Even something simple like "Used by over 10,000 creators worldwide" can dramatically increase conversion.

Finally, we reach **The Call-to-Action (CTA).** The CTA isn't just an ending—it's the emotional crescendo. It should summarize desire, remove hesitation, and offer clear direction. The best CTAs feel like invitations, not orders. "Start your next chapter today," "Try it risk-free," or "Let's build your next breakthrough together" all evoke movement. In AI prompting, specify: *"Write a CTA that inspires action with emotion and clarity, not pressure."*

When you blend these elements—Hook, Story, Solution, Proof, CTA—you create an ad that mirrors human decision-making: curiosity → connection → clarity → confidence → commitment. AI can help maintain this sequence with structured prompts like:

> "Write a 150-word Facebook ad following this structure: emotional hook, short relatable story, clear benefit-driven solution, one credibility line, and a motivational call-to-action."

This kind of architectural instruction allows AI to build persuasive flow automatically, freeing you to focus on creativity and refinement. Advanced copywriters take this even further with **micro-conversion layering**—embedding small "yes" moments throughout the ad. Words like *imagine, what if, picture this,* and *ready?* subtly invite agreement. Each small yes builds momentum toward the final big yes: the click, the sign-up, or the purchase. You can tell AI to include "agreement phrasing" or "momentum questions" to maintain emotional movement.

Remember, conversion isn't manipulation—it's clarity meeting desire. When done ethically, it feels like guidance, not persuasion. Your ad becomes a journey where the reader feels seen, inspired, and ready. In a world full of noise, structure is your signal. When AI helps you design that signal with precision, your words stop being content—they become architecture that sells for you, day and night.

### *How Jason Created AI Ads That Sold Themselves*

Julian had spent years writing ads by instinct. He could feel when a headline worked, when a caption clicked, when a CTA landed—but lately, instinct wasn't enough. Competition was fierce. His clients demanded measurable conversions, not creative intuition. "We love your style," one client said, "but we need predictability." The word hit him like a challenge. Predictability. He realized he needed a structure—a framework that made great ads repeatable, not random.

He began studying high-performing campaigns, analyzing everything from global brands to viral indie ads. It didn't take long to see the pattern: every winning ad followed a rhythm. Hook. Story. Solution. Proof. Call-to-action. Different industries, same architecture. It was like discovering the blueprint to persuasion. Excited, Julian opened his AI writing tool and typed his first structural prompt: *"Write a Facebook ad for a course that helps freelancers find clients, following this structure: emotional hook, short relatable story, benefit-driven solution, proof line, and call-to-action."*

The AI responded: *"You're one email away from your next client—you just don't know how to write it. I used to feel invisible too, sending pitch after pitch with no reply. Then I learned how to write emails that sell without selling. Over 5,000 freelancers have already used this system to land work they love. Ready to be next?"*

Julian smiled. It wasn't just good—it was *complete*. The flow, the emotion, the momentum—it felt effortless. He tested the ad. Within a week, click-through rates tripled. The client called, ecstatic. "It's like you're inside people's heads," she said. Julian laughed quietly. "Not me," he thought. "It's the architecture."

Over the next few months, he began refining the process. He discovered that the most powerful ads didn't sound persuasive—they sounded like clarity. "People don't want to be convinced," he said to a colleague one day. "They want to feel understood." He taught his AI to mimic empathy, to use phrases like "I know what that feels like" and "you're not alone." Suddenly, every ad he wrote felt human again.

One night, working late on a campaign for a personal development brand, Julian took a risk. Instead of listing benefits, he told a story. The ad began: *"I used to hit snooze three times every morning. Not because I was tired—because I was lost. Then one morning, something changed."*

It continued with a simple solution, a line of proof, and a soft CTA: *"If you're ready to stop existing and start living, click below. Your story deserves more chapters."* That ad didn't just convert—it exploded. Tens of thousands of comments, shares, and heartfelt messages poured in. People weren't buying a product; they were buying a narrative they saw themselves in.

As his reputation grew, Julian started teaching other marketers his method. He called it **Conversion Architecture**—the art of designing emotion into sequence. "AI can follow structure," he told his students, "but it's up to you to fill it with soul." He showed them how to prompt for flow, rhythm, and trust-building. He taught them to test micro-moments—the little pauses, the words that make people nod subconsciously. "Every yes counts," he'd say. "Stack enough of them, and the sale is inevitable."

Months later, Julian sat on a stage at a marketing conference, explaining his framework. "The best ads don't push," he said. "They guide. They start as curiosity and end as confidence. That's conversion architecture." The audience erupted in applause.

That night, as he closed his laptop and looked out over the city lights, Julian realized something profound. For years, he'd chased creativity. But the real magic wasn't chaos—it was structure infused with empathy. It wasn't about selling; it was about leading someone home to a decision they already wanted to make.

He whispered to himself, "AI builds the walls. Emotion opens the door."

And with that, he smiled—knowing he'd finally built a framework that could turn words into impact, and impact into freedom.

# Chapter 10: From Automation to Emotion (The Future of AI Copywriting)

We are standing at the crossroads of creativity and computation. The copywriter of the future isn't just a storyteller; they are a strategist of emotion powered by data. AI has changed the way we write, test, and scale marketing—but it hasn't changed why we write. The purpose remains the same: to move people. Every ad, caption, and headline still exists to make someone *feel something enough to act*. The difference is that now, you have a machine capable of amplifying that human intention a thousandfold. The future of AI copywriting will belong to those who blend empathy with engineering—those who can write with both heart and algorithmic precision.

For years, marketers feared AI would replace creativity. Instead, it's become its greatest ally. Artificial intelligence removes the friction of creation—it handles the mechanics so humans can focus on meaning. It drafts, tests, and optimizes at speeds that used to take weeks. But automation without emotion is empty. The true advantage isn't speed; it's *scalability of empathy*. With AI, you can speak personally to millions—each reader feeling like you wrote only for them.

The new era of copywriting revolves around **emotional intelligence at scale.** Every sentence you generate with AI should answer three silent questions your reader always asks: *Do you see me? Do you understand me? Do you care?* When your copy satisfies those three needs, conversion becomes natural. It's no longer about manipulation; it's resonance. Prompt your AI to understand intent, context, and emotion. Instead of "Write an ad to sell a course," say, "Write an ad that inspires self-belief in someone who feels stuck." The difference is the difference between information and inspiration.

The next major evolution is **contextual adaptation.** Modern AI systems can now adjust tone, language, and imagery based on user demographics, psychology, and behavior. You can prompt them to "Write for a 25-year-old creative looking for freedom" or "Speak to a 50-year-old business owner who values legacy." Each version keeps your core message but shifts the emotional frequency. This is marketing personalization at its highest form—empathetic automation.

To stay ahead, you must also master **AI-human collaboration.** Let AI do what it does best—analyze, organize, and optimize—but let your humanity guide the story. Use AI to generate 10 versions of an idea, but trust your instinct to choose the one that *feels right.* Creativity isn't dying; it's being upgraded. You're not competing with

AI—you're conducting it. Think of yourself as a creative composer directing an orchestra of algorithms. Your prompts are your instruments, and emotion is your melody.

One of the most exciting trends emerging from AI-driven marketing is **predictive creativity**—the ability to forecast emotional response before publishing. Tools can now analyze linguistic tone, pacing, and word sentiment to predict engagement. This gives you unprecedented feedback before your ad ever goes live. But as powerful as that is, never forget that emotion isn't mathematical. It's spontaneous, imperfect, and beautifully human. Leave space for that imperfection. The cracks in logic are where authenticity breathes.

Looking ahead, the copywriters who thrive will be those who create emotional systems, not just single ads. They'll use AI to build funnels of empathy—messages that guide readers across stages of awareness, trust, and action seamlessly. You'll move from one-time campaigns to living ecosystems of persuasion that learn, evolve, and grow with your audience.

The real secret of future-proof marketing isn't just knowing how to use AI; it's knowing how to make AI *feel.* When your words combine the precision of technology with the pulse of humanity, you'll create marketing that not only converts but also connects. The algorithms will change. The platforms will change. But emotion—the desire to be understood—will never change.

The future isn't automation replacing art. The future is automation serving art. And those who master that balance will not only dominate the marketplace—they'll redefine it.

### *When Eli Went From Automation to Emotion*

Eli was one of the first copywriters in his firm to embrace AI. When others scoffed, he saw possibility. While they spent hours drafting and revising, he built prompts that could produce polished ads in minutes. But after the initial thrill faded, something bothered him. His campaigns worked—but they didn't *move* people. The metrics were strong, but the comments felt hollow. "Great ad," people wrote, but no one said, "This changed how I feel."

One night, he sat in his apartment overlooking the city skyline, his laptop glowing in the dark. He whispered to himself, "I'm writing faster, but not deeper." He opened his AI assistant and typed a new kind of command: *"Write an ad that helps someone believe in themselves again."*

The response was quiet but powerful: *"You don't need another plan. You need to remember who you are."*

Eli froze. It wasn't flashy—it was honest. He tested it on a small campaign for a personal development brand. Within days, messages poured in. People weren't talking about the product—they were thanking him for the words. "This ad made me cry," one wrote. Another said, "I needed this today."

That night, Eli realized what had been missing all along: *heart*. AI could write, but it couldn't *care*. Only he could provide that. From then on, he used AI differently. He treated it like a collaborator, not a replacement. He fed it stories, emotions, and lived experiences. "Write this like someone who's been through failure and found hope again," he'd say. The results were extraordinary. His ads became conversations. His audience grew. His brand exploded.

Soon, Eli began teaching others his process. He called it "Heartwired Copywriting." In workshops, he told his students, "AI gives you speed, but only you give it soul." He taught them how to blend emotional storytelling with AI precision. One student, a shy freelancer, later wrote him to say, "Your system gave me my first viral campaign—and my confidence back." That message meant more to him than any paycheck.

One year later, Eli was invited to speak at a global marketing summit. The audience was packed with executives, creators, and AI enthusiasts. On stage, he looked out at the crowd and said, "We used to fear AI would take our jobs. But what it's really doing is forcing us to rediscover our humanity." The room fell silent. He continued, "AI doesn't replace us—it remembers us. It takes our best ideas, our deepest emotions, and carries them further than we could alone."

He paused, smiled, and added, "The future isn't man or machine. It's both, working together to tell the stories that need to be told."

As the applause filled the room, Eli thought back to the night he'd stared at his empty screen, wondering if creativity still mattered. Now he knew. The future didn't belong to those who wrote faster—it belonged to those who wrote *truer*.

Later that evening, back at his desk, Eli opened a blank document. The city lights flickered below as he typed his final note to himself: *"Never let the machine write without your heart guiding it."*

He leaned back and smiled. The cursor blinked at the end of the sentence—a heartbeat on the page. And for the first time in years, he felt completely certain: the future of copywriting was not about replacing emotion with automation. It was about teaching automation how to feel.

# Epilogue

*The Human Spark: Writing the Future With AI*

The world of marketing has always been a reflection of humanity itself—a dance between logic and longing, between what we sell and what we believe. In the beginning, advertising was persuasion in its simplest form: a person with a message, trying to reach another person's heart. Decades later, as screens multiplied and attention spans shrank, that same mission remained. Now, standing in an era defined by artificial intelligence, we find ourselves returning full circle. The tools have changed, but the soul of communication has not. It's still about *connection*.

AI has taught us something profound about ourselves. It's shown that creativity isn't just about invention—it's about translation. Every great ad, story, or message is an act of translation: turning emotion into language, experience into words, and vision into action. AI is simply another translator—one that moves at the speed of thought. It listens, learns, and generates, but it doesn't *feel*. It can imitate emotion but not originate it. That power still belongs to you—the creator, the empath, the dreamer behind the keyboard.

Throughout this book, you've learned that great copywriting isn't about tricks or templates. It's about empathy expressed through structure. You've learned that emotion can be modeled, curiosity can be coded, and brand voice can be taught—but compassion cannot be automated. The art of AI copywriting is the art of partnership. The machine offers clarity, precision, and speed. You bring the soul. Together, you don't just make ads—you craft experiences that move through screens and into hearts.

There's an old saying in storytelling: *"The most powerful stories are the ones that tell the truth we've been too afraid to say."* That truth is what AI can't replicate. It can predict patterns, but it can't feel the pulse of insecurity before success, the bittersweet ache of nostalgia, or the quiet courage of someone deciding to try again. That's where you come in. Every time you sit down to write—whether for a product, a brand, or a cause—you're not just shaping perception. You're offering hope in words.

In the next era of advertising, authenticity will no longer be optional. People have grown immune to manipulation, resistant to noise, and allergic to exaggeration. What they crave is meaning. AI allows you to deliver that meaning faster, more personally, and at scale—but meaning itself must be real. The future of copywriting won't be defined by the best algorithm, but by the best *intent*. Imagine what this means for you. You now have the ability to write for millions in minutes, to translate emotion across languages and cultures instantly, and to tell stories that resonate in every corner of the digital world. You're no longer limited by time or resources. The bottleneck isn't the tool—it's the depth of your empathy. Every time you give AI a better prompt, you're giving it a better version of yourself to amplify. In that sense, AI doesn't make writing less human; it makes humanity more visible.

Think of what comes next. Entire brands will be born from single sentences. Campaigns will adapt themselves in real time, shifting tone and story as data flows in. But amid that precision, the greatest currency will remain emotional truth. The brands that lead the future won't just be efficient—they'll be *alive*. They'll sound like people who listen, who understand, who care. And behind every one of those voices, there will still be a writer—a human—guiding the machine toward meaning.

Perhaps the greatest lesson in this journey is that technology doesn't define us; we define it. You now hold a tool that can multiply your creativity infinitely. What you choose to do with it will shape the stories the world hears next. Will you use it to create noise—or to create resonance? Will you automate repetition—or amplify revelation? The future is being written in real time, and your words are the ink. Close your eyes for a moment and imagine this: someone, somewhere, will one day read an ad you wrote with AI and feel seen for the first time. They'll whisper, "That's me." They'll click, not because they were persuaded, but because they were *understood*. That's not marketing—that's impact. That's what happens when automation and emotion meet in perfect rhythm.

So as you finish this book, remember—AI may be your assistant, but *you* are the author. You are the voice behind the vision, the feeling behind the formula, the spark that turns systems into stories. The world doesn't need more noise. It needs more truth, more empathy, more creators who lead with heart and craft with intelligence.

Write boldly. Prompt with purpose. Speak as if the world is listening—because now, it is.

The future of AI copywriting doesn't belong to machines. It belongs to *those who teach machines how to speak human.*

And that, dear reader, is where your story begins.

www.ingramcontent.com/pod-product-compliance
Lightning Source LLC
LaVergne TN
LVHW022015200926
848481LV00007B/2411
* 9 7 9 8 2 9 5 4 2 3 3 4 5 *